TABLE OF CONTENTS

CHAPTER 1

HI, BUTTERFLY!

Colorful wings flap. Long, smooth **antennas** feel the air. This **insect** is a great Mormon butterfly!

antenna

ALL ABOUT INSECTS

ALL ABOUT BUTTERFLIES

by Karen Latchana Kenney

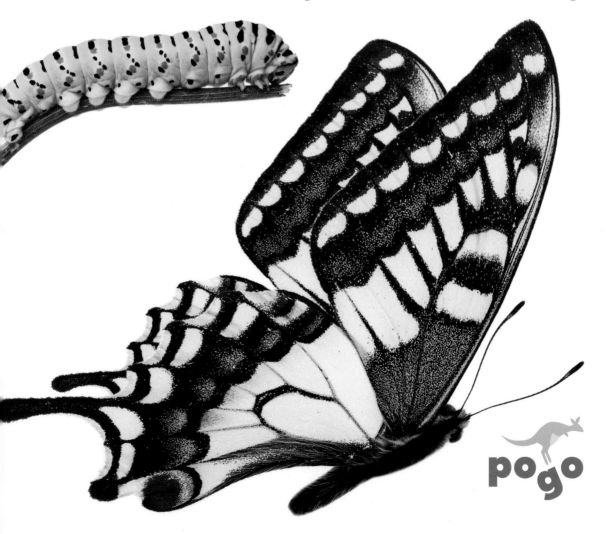

pogo

Ideas for Parents and Teachers

Pogo Books let children practice reading informational text while introducing them to nonfiction features such as headings, labels, sidebars, maps, and diagrams, as well as a table of contents, glossary, and index.

Carefully leveled text with a strong photo match offers early fluent readers the support they need to succeed.

Before Reading

- "Walk" through the book and point out the various nonfiction features. Ask the student what purpose each feature serves.
- Look at the glossary together. Read and discuss the words.

Read the Book

- Have the child read the book independently.
- Invite him or her to list questions that arise from reading.

After Reading

- Discuss the child's questions. Talk about how he or she might find answers to those questions.
- Prompt the child to think more. Ask: Have you ever seen a butterfly? Where was it? What did its wings look like?

Pogo Books are published by Jump!
5357 Penn Avenue South
Minneapolis, MN 55419
www.jumplibrary.com

Copyright © 2024 Jump!
International copyright reserved in all countries.
No part of this book may be reproduced in any form without written permission from the publisher.

Library of Congress Cataloging-in-Publication Data

Names: Kenney, Karen Latchana, author.
Title: All about butterflies / by Karen Latchana Kenney.
Description: Minneapolis, MN: Jump!, Inc., [2024]
Series: All about insects | Includes index.
Audience: Ages 7-10
Identifiers: LCCN 2022048364 (print)
LCCN 2022048365 (ebook)
ISBN 9798885244275 (hardcover)
ISBN 9798885244282 (paperback)
ISBN 9798885244299 (ebook)
Subjects: LCSH: Butterflies—Juvenile literature.
Classification: LCC QL544.2 .K464 2024 (print)
LCC QL544.2 (ebook)
DDC 595.78/9—dc23/eng/20221024
LC record available at https://lccn.loc.gov/2022048364
LC ebook record available at https://lccn.loc.gov/2022048365

Editor: Jenna Gleisner
Designer: Emma Almgren-Bersie

Photo Credits: KRIACHKO OLEKSII/Shutterstock, cover, 3; Anest/Shutterstock, 1 (left); Butterfly Hunter/Shutterstock, 1 (right); Matee Nuserm/Dreamstime, 4; Off_abstract/Shutterstock, 5; Andreas HÄuslbetz/Dreamstime, 6-7; Wirestock/iStock, 8-9; SusanWoodImages/iStock, 10; imageBROKER/Alamy, 11; Sarah2/Dreamstime, 12-13; LaSalle-Photo/iStock, 14-15; panda3800/Shutterstock, 16; Vojtaheroutcom/Dreamstime, 17; Jag_cz/Shutterstock, 18-19; Susan Hodgson/Alamy, 20-21; Matee Nuserm/Shutterstock, 23.

Printed in the United States of America at Corporate Graphics in North Mankato, Minnesota.

head

thorax

abdomen

wing

All butterflies have three main body parts. They are a head, a thorax, and an abdomen. Their bodies and two sets of wings are covered in colorful **scales**. They make bright patterns.

Butterflies start out as eggs. They hatch as caterpillars. Caterpillars eat a lot of food to grow. Most eat one or a few kinds of plants. Monarch butterfly caterpillars only eat milkweed plants. Large White caterpillars eat cauliflower plant leaves.

Large White caterpillar

TAKE A LOOK!

Butterflies grow in four stages. Take a look!

1. A butterfly starts as a tiny egg.

2. A **larva** hatches from each egg. It is a caterpillar. It eats and grows.

3. The caterpillar makes a **chrysalis**. It is now a **pupa**. Its body changes.

4. It comes out of the chrysalis as an adult butterfly.

Adult butterflies drink their food. A butterfly's **proboscis** uncurls. It sucks **nectar** from flowers. Butterflies also drink liquids from old, soft fruits.

proboscis

CHAPTER 2

STAYING SAFE

Look at the underside of this milkweed plant's leaves. What do you see? It is a monarch butterfly egg. Butterflies lay eggs where their larvae will have food. They hide their eggs in places that are hard to see.

egg

Caterpillars make tasty meals for birds and other **predators**. To stay safe, some caterpillars blend in. A giant swallowtail caterpillar looks like bird poop.

giant swallowtail caterpillar

silk tent

Some caterpillars make their own homes. Small tortoiseshell caterpillars live on nettle plants. Their bodies make silk.

The caterpillars build a web of silk into a tent. They stay safe together under their tent.

DID YOU KNOW?

A caterpillar makes silk from a tube by its mouth. The silk is liquid when it comes out. It turns into solid string when it touches air.

Some butterflies have colors or patterns that keep them safe. Owl butterflies have spots on their wings. They look like owl eyes. Birds leave them alone.

DID YOU KNOW?

Some butterflies gather in groups to stay safe. Zebra butterflies **roost** together each night. They wake each other in the morning. How? They bump into one another.

owl butterfly

CHAPTER 3

STRONG WINGS

Butterflies flap their wings to fly. Each wing is thinner than a fingernail. The wings catch air like kites. This allows butterflies to glide through the air.

pollen

Their strong wings take butterflies from flower to flower. Butterflies spread the **pollen** they collect. Plants use pollen to make seeds.

Butterfly wings can also take them high. Some butterflies fly above mountains. Monarch butterflies can fly higher than the clouds.

The blue morpho butterfly lives in the Amazon Rain Forest. Airplane pilots have seen them flying above the tallest trees!

blue morpho
butterfly

painted lady
butterflies

Some butterflies **migrate**. They fly thousands of miles to better temperatures. Their wings may be torn and worn when they arrive. Painted lady butterflies fly the longest distance. They fly from Africa to the Arctic Circle!

Butterflies are strong insects. Have you seen one fly?

DID YOU KNOW?

More than 17,000 kinds of butterflies fly around the world. The only place they do not live is Antarctica.

ACTIVITIES & TOOLS

GROW A BUTTERFLY PLANT

Monarch butterflies only eat milkweed. Grow milkweed to help them find food with this fun activity!

What You Need:
- empty cardboard egg carton
- scissors
- metal or plastic tray
- potting soil
- milkweed seeds
- water

❶ Cut off the top half of the egg carton. Poke a hole in the bottom of each cup.

❷ Set the carton in a tray. Then fill each cup with potting soil.

❸ Place one seed in each cup. Add a little more soil to cover it.

❹ Drip some water in each cup. Place the tray near a window that gets sunlight.

❺ Observe your plants. Add some water each day. Make sure the soil does not dry out. Soon, seedlings will sprout.

❻ Once the seedlings grow big, cut the cups apart. Plant some cups outside. Give the others to friends or family members to plant!

antennas: Feelers on the head of an insect.

chrysalis: A hard cover made by a butterfly larva to protect itself.

insect: A small animal with three pairs of legs, one or two pairs of wings, and three main body parts.

larva: An insect in the stage of growth between egg and pupa.

migrate: To move to another area or climate at a particular time of year.

nectar: A sweet liquid made by flowers.

pollen: Tiny yellow grains in flowers that plants need to make seeds.

predators: Animals that hunt other animals for food.

proboscis: A long, tubelike mouthpart that helps butterflies suck nectar.

pupa: An insect in the stage of growth between larva and adult.

roost: To settle somewhere to rest or sleep.

scales: Thin, flat, overlapping pieces.

TO LEARN MORE

Finding more information is as easy as 1, 2, 3.

❶ **Go to www.factsurfer.com**

❷ **Enter "butterflies" into the search box.**

❸ **Choose your book to see a list of websites.**

FACT SURFER